P9-BYD-781

The Complete Book of Unusual Names

The Complete Book of Unusual Names

When you don't want to sound the same, look here for names beyond Joe, Jim and Jane

Daniel David

CHAMPION PRESS, LTD.
WISCONSIN

CHAMPION PRESS, LTD.
BELGIUM, WISCONSIN
Copyright © 2006 Daniel David

All rights reserved. No part of this book shall be reproduced, stored, or transmitted by any means without written permission from the publisher. Although every precaution has been taken in the preparation of this book, the publisher and author assume no responsibility for errors or omissions. Neither is any liability assumed for damages resulting from the use of the information contained herein. For more information contact: Champion Press, Ltd. 765 Main Street, Belgium, WI 53004 or call toll-free 877-250-3354.

Reasonable care has been taken in the preparation of the text to insure its clarity and accuracy. The book is sold with the understanding that the author and publisher are not engaged in rendering professional service. The author and publisher specifically disclaim any liability, loss or risk, personal or otherwise, which is incurred as a consequence, directly or indirectly, of the use and application of any of the contents of this book.

ISBN: 1932783296
LCCN: 2004115190

Manufactured in the United States of America

10 9 8 7 6 5

3 6645 00049962 4

Dedicated to
My Parents
Venetka & Narsai David

A few notes from the author

- The names are not divided by gender; many of the names can be used for either sex.

- Preferred pronunciation is shown in parenthesis.

- Each first name is shown with a middle and/or last name to emphasize the importance of the marriage between all of the names.

INTRODUCTION

You hold in your hands a book bursting with unique and exciting names. The author has compiled a list of names that you won't find in any other books on the baby name shelf. Some roll off your tongue, some bounce, and some even tap dance. Most, such as **Visolo** and **Koria**, you've never heard before. Others — **Achilles**, **Pierot** — are names that rarely get used today. And still others, such as **Blue** and **Sash**, are words that you've heard in another context, but never would have considered naming your child. **Try thinking of names in a new way.** Don't worry about out-of-date definitions. Try thinking of a name as a dash of color you give to the world; a way to leave your mark, like an elaborate scarf wound through auburn hair, or a periwinkle, paisley tie that everyone admires. You might even find yourself inspired to take one of these names for yourself, not just for your baby!

When you go through this book to find the unique name that's right for your needs, you'll notice that there are no definitions. Why limit yourself by antiquated, arbitrary definitions which in the end, have nothing to do with the child who bears the name? How important is it that Gertrude means "warrior woman" and Michael means "godlike"? Not very. Often a name can mean two different things, maybe "leader" in one language, and "prickly cactus" in another. If you knew that Marion meant "bitter", would you refrain from using it even if it were your favorite name in the world? Of course the meaning wouldn't matter if your heart was set on it. That's why you'll find names on this list which either have no meaning at all or have meaning in another context. It's not important that **Guage** can't be translated. It's not important that **Ajax** can be used in the kitchen and **Minnow** is a fish. **What matters is that you like the name.** Consider going by instinct and choosing names simply because you like the sound! It's okay to trust yourself. You have a creative impulse inside that can guide you to the right name.

Every name we use today has a source. Someone somewhere created each one, and in so doing, added their legacy to our language. At the root of every name lies a spark of inspiration. Now it's your turn to be the author of a name. As parents, who you are as creative individuals will live on in your child. Your personality will be reflected in their name. Giving your children a name from this book will set them apart from all those Elizabeths and Johns. Their name will illuminate their identity in a special way, granting them uniqueness in an overwhelmingly anonymous world. While all the Michaels huddle in a crowd, **Hockney** will glow; **Isola** will sparkle.

Remember, you can always pick a name from this book only as a middle name. If you simply adore the name **Chimmney** but can't bring yourself to use it as a first name, consider calling your kid Jason Chimmney Parker. When he gets tired of common old Jason, he can ask people to start calling him Chimmney. Or you can call your child an unusual first name, but give them a more standard middle name. How about Pasha Jane Sinclair? If she doesn't like being Pasha, she can always use Jane among her peers. There are so many options in the naming process!

Every person with a weird name can tell funny stories about navigating the world with it. They have to repeat it for strangers; they have to spell it out loud; they get called other names or strange hybrids. Kids might snicker or make up nicknames for them. But they can also recount the rewarding experiences that their inventive name has brought them. Every time they have to spell or repeat their name to a stranger, they open the door into a conversation with someone they would not have ordinarily talked to. Every time their name gets mispronounced, they get asked curious questions and are paid extra attention. And, every time someone dubs them a funny nickname, they also receive countless compliments from those conventionally named folks who covet their originality. They might even find that an unusual name benefits them in ways they never could have imagined. Consider what happened to a small girl with a peculiar name on the first day of school:

Mr. O'Neill swayed slowly from the heels to the balls of his feet; his thick, stubby fingers grasping firmly to either side of the faux-wood podium. With jowls and a mouth set like a bulldog, he fixed his hard eyes of the seventh grade class and called the roll on this first day of school. One little girl sat tensely, waiting for her strange name to come booming across the classroom. Mr.

O'Neill was already at the M's.

"Jennifer Morris!" he bellowed.

A hand crept slowly up. "Here", peeped a girl a few chairs ahead.

"Adam O'Connor."

A tough guy slouching in his seat muttered, "Yeh, here..."

"Sit up straight!" ordered Mr. O'Neill. The boy snapped to attention.

"Laura Parks."

"Present," whispered someone in the back row.

"Speak up! barked the teacher.

"Pre...present," spoke the voice, a tad bit louder.

Suddenly, Mr. O'Neill fell silent. He was staring intently at his roll call sheet, so intently that the whole class could see the top of his head and the circle near the back where his military regime haircut grew sparse. He kept staring down at the page. Tiny beads of sweat gathered at his temples. His fingers drummed nervously on the podium. With his right hand, he yanked at his brown, polyester pants. His nose twitched. A minute passed. The class began to stir. What could be the matter?

The little girl knew she was the only one who could help him.

"Um, I think the next one, it might be me," she stammered.

Mr. O'Neill glanced up and looked straight at her.

She spoke: "Lilan... You say Leelawn Pahtree." She looked quickly down at here desk.

Mr. O'Neill paused. And then, for the first time that morning there was a softness in his voice. "Thanks," he muttered humbly. "Lilan." His stern gaze melted. He smiled at her.

She smiled back.

"Kenneth Rogers!" he yelled.

The little girl was me twelve years ago. It wasn't always easy to have this name. But on that day in Mr. O'Neill's class I learned that "Lilan" had a certain power not shared by the Kenneths, Lauras, Adams and Jennifers of the world. To think a name could be funky and ingenious enough to sweeten up even a drill sergeant of a teacher! This book is full of names just like that. Don't confine your offspring to the dull majority. Let **Heron** and **Paradiso** work their magic!

Take a good look at these names. Some you'll laugh at. Some you'll think silly or bizarre. But you may come across a name — either as rare as **Rhone** or as unconventional as **Bilt** — and pause for a second to say, "Hey, I like the sound of that, how cool!" And you may just like it enough to daringly rename yourself or offer your child the gift of an extraordinary name.

Good luck on a lively journey into the fertile world of NAMES, where, from the words and sounds of our surroundings, these names were harvested from the richest of crops. Pleasant pickings!

Lilan Patri

NAMES

A.C.
>Ex: *A.C. Carey Reynolds*

Aalten
>(ALL-TIN)
>Ex: *Aalten Perrin Smith*

Azzarei
>(AS-ARE-AY)
>Ex: *Azzarei Roland Bechtel*

Abacus
>Ex: *Abacus Wen Stevens*

Abile
>(A-BILL)
>Ex: *Abile Maddie Ryanson*

Absinthe
>Ex: *Absinthe Chester Malone*

Acacia
>Ex: *Acacia Rose Sullivan*

Acadia
>Ex: *Acadia Cole Baxter*

Acara
>(AH-CAR-AH)
>Ex: *Acara Nellie Smith*

Acari
>(AH-CAR-IE)
>Ex: *Acari Crosby Stills*

Acaru
>(A-CAR-OO)
>Ex: *Acaru Wills Jameson*

Achilles
>Ex: *Achilles Sample Hellerson*

Achim
>(AH-KEEM)
>Ex: *Achim Allen Lewis*

Acton
>Ex: *Acton Roland Stilles*

Adaline
>Ex: *Adaline Lewis Stevenson*

Adella
>   Ex: *Adella Marie Martinez*

Adina
>   (AH-DEE-NA)
>   Ex: *Adina Rosa Alvarez*

Adlar
>   Ex: *Adlar Allen Jones*

Aeolus
>   (AY-O-LUS)
>   Ex: *Aeolus Whalen Pitman*

Aero
>   Ex: *Aero Jacob Starr*

Aeron
>   (AIR-ON)
>   Ex: *Aeron Nicholas Bailer*

Agius
>   (AY-JUSS)
>   Ex: *Agius Matthew Taylor*

Ahramis
>   (UH-RAY-MISS)
>   Ex: *Ahramis Cole Nexler*

Aileen
>   (AY-LEAN)
>   Ex: *Aileen Vella Stoker*

Ainsley
>   Ex: *Ainsley Paula Matson*

Airel
>   Ex: *Airel Daylin Jones*

Aitor
>   (AY-TORE)
>   Ex: *Aitor Nathan Cain*

Ajax
>   Ex: *Ajax Marcus Weston*

Ake
>   Ex: *Ake Willis Peterson*

Alabama
>   Ex: *Alabama Silvi Dyer*

Aladdin
    Ex: *Aladdin Todd Greene*
Albany
    Ex: *Sue Albany Watson*
Albion
    Ex: *Albion Rice Wexler*
Alcala
    Ex: *Alcala Rivera Beatty*
Alcatraz
    Ex: *Christopher Alcatraz Cobbler*
Aldagrove
    Ex: *Aldagrove Rhen Stevens*
Aldea
    Ex: *Tammy Aldea Farnsworth*
Alder
    Ex: *Alder Bixby Matson*
Aldo
    Ex: *Aldo Allen Courtland*
Alejo
    (AL-AY-HO)
    Ex: *Jake Alejo Stevens*
Alesian
    (AL-EE-SHIN)
    Ex: *Alesian Ramon Vexler*
Alger
    (AL-JUR)
    Ex: *Marcus Alger Callahan*
Algier
    (AL-JEER)
    Ex: *Algier Willis Babcock*
Alinda
    Ex: *Sherry Alinda Bryerson*
Alinka
    Ex: *Karen Alinka Porter*
Alloy
    Ex: *Christian Alloy Miller*

Aloe
    Ex: *Aloe Carey Shores*
Alpha
    Ex: *Alpha Radley Mitchell*
Alpine
    Ex: *Carey Alpine Pearly*
Alta
    Ex: *Paula Alta Graff*
Alton
    Ex: *Tony Alton Greer*
Alves
    Ex: *Richards Alves Thorinton*
Alluma
    Ex: *Alluma Rose Sonning*
Amador
    Ex: *Amador Christian Stilles*
Amaryllis
    Ex: *Amaryllis Christal Sharp*
Amato
    (AH-MA-TOE)
    Ex: *Amato Dale Stevens*
Ambrose
    Ex: *Ambrose Willis Bolton*
Ambrosia
    Ex: *Ambrosia Alysa Waters*
Amerca
    (AH-MARE-KA)
    Ex: *Amerca Jane Sarrison*
America
    Ex: *Samuel America Payton*
Amerigo
    Ex: *Manuel Amerigo Valdez*
Amethyst
    Ex: *Amethyst Raquel Pittford*
Amir
    (AH-MEER)
    Ex: *Jaylin Amir Razzami*

Amos
  Ex: *Vincent Amos Allen*
Andros
  Ex: *Mark Andros Parker*
Anemone
  (AH-NEM-OH-NEE)
  Ex: *Susan Anemone Stone*
Angora
  Ex: *Angora Roxanne Smith*
Anisetta
  Ex: *Roseyln Anisetta Marianos*
Annadale
  Ex: *Annadale Elizabeth Radley*
Anniston
  Ex: *Rex Anniston Portier*
Anselmo
  Ex: *Steven Anselmo Jones*
Antelope
  Ex: *Antelope Ramona Ramirez*
Anthracite
  Ex: *Anthracite Silver Jones*
Antigo
  Ex: *Raull Antigo Santiago*
Antigua
  (ANN-TEE-GWA)
  Ex: *Antigua Susana Callista*
Aoki
  (AY-OH-KEY)
  Ex: *Aoki Gin Roberts*
Aptos
  Ex: *Todd Aptos Wheeler*
Aqua
  Ex: *Aqua Nicole Fisher*
Aquavit
  (AH-KWA-VEET)
  Ex: *Aquavit Cannon Calder*

Arzuela
>   Ex: *Arzuela Mimosa Sorrendo*

Arabian
>   Ex: *Bailey Arabian Buchannan*

Aragon
>   (AIR-AH-GONE)
>   Ex: *Aragon Carrey Smith*

Aram
>   Ex: *Aram Craig Aiken*

Arca
>   Ex: *Arca Suzanne Walton*

Arcy
>   Ex: *Alexandria Arcy Courtland*

Arena
>   Ex: *Arena Michelle Gainor*

Argent
>   Ex: *Samuel Argent Taylor*

Arglyle
>   Ex: *Susan Arglye Smith*

Arkansas
>   Ex: *Jack Arkansas Swensen*

Arleta
>   (AR-LET-TA)
>   Ex: *Tania Arleta Weston*

Arley
>   Ex: *Arley Cole Thompson*

Armitage
>   Ex: *Jane Armitage Sansome*

Artic
>   Ex: *Artic Rail Cogsworth*

Artino
>   Ex: *Artino Ricardo Sails*

Aruba
>   Ex: *Donna Aruba Gates*

Arvada
>   (AR-VAY-DA)
>   Ex: *Corrina Arvada Ramirez*

Arzat
    Ex: *Arzat Thomas Smith*
Arzuela
    Ex: *Arzuela Mimosa Sorrendo*
Ashby
    Ex: *Ashby Nicole Street*
Asher
    Ex: *Johnny Asher Baker*
Ashford
    Ex: *Ashford Rex Billings*
Ashlan
    Ex: *Rachel Ashlan Tiddings*
Ashur
    Ex: *Ashur Graecano*
Ashwood
    Ex: *Paul Ashwood Sandler*
Asta
    Ex: *Asta Jones*
Aster
    Ex: *Aster Pixley Robertson*
Astin
    Ex: *Vespa Astin Pelligrini*
Astor
    Ex: *Kim Astor Rogers*
Astron
    Ex: *Rex Astron Evanston*
Athens
    Ex: *Tamara Athens Rosenthal*
Atkin
    Ex: *Atkin Torrence Jackson*
Atlanta
    Ex: *Atlanta Lynn Stevenson*
Atlantic
    Ex: *Robert Atlantic Cain*
Atlin
    Ex: *Toby Atlin James*
Atmos
    Ex: *Atmos Ryan Mattson*

Attalla
 Ex: *Erica Attalla Ryerson*
Aubin
 (OH-BIN)
 Ex: *Aubin Jones*
Auborn
 Ex: *Jane Auborn Sinclair*
Aurora
 Ex: *Nina Aurora Stevenson*
Ava
 (AY-VA)
 Ex: *Ava Han Georgia Lee*
Avalon
 Ex: *Rick Avalon Sampson*
Avant
 (AH-VAHNT)
 Ex: *Avant Marina Jacard*
Avedon
 (AH-VEH-DAWN)
 Ex: *Zane Avedon Spear*
Avenida
 Ex: *Avenida Laura Smith*
Avian
 Ex: *Alexis Avian Kimball*
Avianca
 (AH-VI-ON-KA)
 Ex: *Avianca Ambrose Sanchez*
Avila
 (AH-VEE-LA)
 Ex: *Lexi Avila McKinney*
Avin
 Ex: *Avin Gerrund Jones*
Avion
 Ex: *Alexander Avion Ail*
Avirita
 Ex: *Avirita Rose*

Avondale
> Ex: *Zachery Avondale Spencer*

Avril
> Ex: *Avril Peters*

Axel
> Ex: *Axel Sin Joiner*

Axis
> Ex: *Axis Mary Marino*

Ay
> Ex: *Ay Perry Rizen*

Ayala
> (I-ALL-A)
> Ex: *Ayala Donna Moore*

Ayenee
> Ex: *Ayenee Sara McNair*

Ayler
> Ex: *Ayler Ryland Sloan*

Aylor
> Ex: *Rick Aylor Bekins*

Aymax
> Ex: *Roufus Aymax Bixler*

Ayr
> Ex: *Tom Ayr Wexler*

Azalia
> Ex: *Azalia Ann Burlin*

Azevedo
> (AS-EH-VAY-DOE)
> Ex: *Bobby Azevedo Anders*

Azores
> Ex: *Azores Evan Cole*

B
Ex: *B Waitlin Mines*

Baba
Ex: *Baba Haddad*

Bacall
Ex: *Bacall Betsy Peterson*

Bacardi
Ex: *Barcardi Willis Jenkins*

Baffin
Ex: *Sam Baffin Wilson*

Bahama
Ex: *Andreas Bahama Cooper*

Bailen
Ex: *Bailen Moore Ryerson*

Baja
Ex: *Jack Baja Dune*

Balboa
Ex: *Lisa Balboa Walton*

Balen
(BAA-LEN)
Ex: *Balen Michael Gore*

Balentine
Ex: *Stephanie Balentine Diamond*

Ballon
Ex: *Panther Ballon Phillips*

Baltic
Ex: *Baltic Jones*

Bamboo
Ex: *Bamboo Soren Sinclair*

Banbury
Ex: *Sarah Banbury Wills*

Bancroft
Ex: *Bancroft Jerrund Beales*

Bandelaire
Ex: *Ricky Bandelaire Borrinson*

Banguard
Ex: *Morris Banguard Walker*

Banks
Ex: *Banks Cohen Fisher*
Baptiste
Ex: *Jean Baptiste Mission*
Barbados
Ex: *Malcolm Barbados Michner*
Barbano
(BAR-BAH-NO)
Ex: *Vince Barbano Bail*
Barbee
Ex: *Barbee Bell*
Barbera
Ex: *Jules Barbera Cox*
Barbuda
Ex: *Barbuda Bronks*
Bareen
Ex: *Bareen Velopes Indio*
Barn
Ex: *Barn Barron Gainor*
Barnum
Ex: *Bill Barnum Staples*
Bartel
Ex: *Marcus Bartel DelSanto*
Bartlett
Ex: *Sarah Bartlett Pearson*
Barton
Ex: *Christopher Barton Steele*
Baru
Ex: *Spaniel Baru Jones*
Basco
Ex: *Dwayne Basco Price*
Bassett
Ex: *Silvia Bassett Akeman*
Bassie
Ex: *Bassie Monroe*
Batelin
Ex: *Lisa Batelin Robins*

Bates

    Ex: *Aurthur Bates Topella*

Batori

    Ex: *Batori Norland*

Bautista

    Ex: *Bautista Parker Burns*

Bax

    Ex: *Bax Taylin*

Bayaka

    Ex: *Cindy Bayaka Sanderson*

Baye

    Ex: *Baye Seton Wallace*

Bayes

    Ex: *Bayes d'Or Railand*

Baylor

    Ex: *Baylor Lane Bexler*

Beacon

    Ex: *Beacon Todd Silver*

Beale

    Ex: *Beale Sarrington Moore*

Bechor

    (BECK-OR)

    Ex: *Bechor John*

Bechtel

    Ex: *Phoebe Bechtel Sails*

Becker

    Ex: *Shelby Becker Willits*

Beech

    Ex: *Brandon Beech Tillman*

Beeini

    (BEE-EN-EE)

    Ex: *Beeini Sales Cartwright*

Beem

    Ex: *Nicholas Beem Price*

Beienel

    (BEE-EN-ELLE)

    Ex: *Beienel Stevens*

Beijing
   Ex: *Beijing Li Thompson*
Belaire
   Ex: *Spencer Belaire Robbins*
Beldin
   Ex: *Robert Beldin Stark*
Beldon
   Ex: *Macy Beldon Clark*
Belize
   Ex: *Elizabeth Belize Brighton*
Belmont
   Ex: *Belmont Sheraton*
Beltine
   Ex: *Jason Beltine Walker*
Belvedere
   Ex: *Belvedere Marie Presley*
Benbow
   Ex: *Rodney Benbow Rodriguiz*
Bendel
   Ex: *Bendel Wyman Wilks*
Bendix
   Ex: *Bendix Ruben Parker*
Bennet
   Ex: *Jessica Bennet Fox*
Bengal
   Ex: *Bengal Lloyd Webster*
Bento
   Ex: *John Bento Price*
Benton
   Ex: *Benton Wayne Wilson*
Beo
   Ex: *Beo Connor Millens*
Beowolf
   Ex: *Charles Beowolf Excaliber*
Berent
   Ex: *William Berent Brice*

Bergen
Ex: *Bergen Tye Sallinger*
Bering
Ex: *Bering Nealand Solari*
Beringer
Ex: *Thomas Beringer Appleby*
Berman
Ex: *Victor Berman Johnson*
Beston
Ex: *Chet Beston Bearman*
Beta
Ex: *Randolf Beta Chartes*
Bexley
Ex: *Bexley Avin Moore*
Bicksley
Ex: *Bicksley Trevor Holmes*
Billings
Ex: *Darrin Billings Connors*
Bilt
Ex: *Bilt Steven Ryerson*
Biltmore
Ex: *Biltmore Jackson Bird*
Bioletti
Ex: *Jacqueline Bioletti Smith*
Bionda
Ex: *Bionda Paisley Grey*
Birley
Ex: *Birley Blithe Halloway*
Birmingham
Ex: *Carla Birmingham Barthe*
Bisbee
Ex: *Ona Bisbee Dale*
Bisco
Ex: *Bisco May Peerman*
Bisquo
Ex: *Jay Bisquo Pierce*

Bizou
> Ex: *Lola Bizou Branca*

Bjork
> Ex: *Bjork Conrad Skores*

Bobo
> Ex: *Bobo Jack Rillin*

Bogard
> Ex: *Gallen Bogard Giles*

Bogie
> Ex: *Bogie Anders Cole*

Bolero
> Ex: *Sam Bolero Bryerson*

Bolinger
> Ex: *Chloe Bolinger Bricks*

Bolt
> Ex: *Bolt Sheldon*

Bolton
> Ex: *Wilks Bolton Kellen*

Bombay
> Ex: *Salina Bombay Junips*

Bond
> Ex: *Bond Era Ricks*

Bonsai
> Ex: *Jerret Bonsai Kale*

Bonta
> Ex: *Shirley Bonta Kaye*

Booth
> Ex: *Booth Ales Wilt*

Bora
> Ex: *Bora Bora Bronks*

Bordean
> Ex: *Bordean Rice Becker*

Bosch
> Ex: *Bosch Hollis*

Bose
> (BOZE)
> Ex: *Bose Allison Rand*

Boston
> Ex: *Leo Boston Varella*

Bourne
> Ex: *Leonard Bourne Balice*

Bova
> Ex: *Bova Reeves*

Bovo
> Ex: *Bovo Richards Gellin*

Boxer
> Ex: *Boxer Cravates*

Bracano
> Ex: *Julio Bracano Broussard*

Braemar
> Ex: *Braemar Lindo Fierendino*

Brahm
> Ex: *Brahm Riley Santos*

Brando
> Ex: *Tare Brando Shields*

Branwyn
> Ex: *Jill Branwyn Pinkerton*

Brazen
> Ex: *Brazen Rich Evans*

Bree
> Ex: *Carla Bree Seens*

Brekken
> Ex: *Brekken Stiles Tate*

Bremen
> Ex: *Vic Bremen Goldman*

Bremmen
> Ex: *Youri Bremmen Volcari*

Breton
> Ex: *Breton Morecroft*

Brewster
> Ex: *Milvin Brewster Phillips*

Briar
> Ex: *Leena Briar Sorrinson*

Briarcliff
　　Ex: *Eric Briarcliff Staten*
Brice
　　Ex: *Brice Marina Hane*
Brick
　　Ex: *Brick Conrad Fishell*
Bricka
　　Ex: *Bricka Lesley Thomas*
Bridges
　　Ex: *Madison Bridges Wright*
Brighton
　　Ex: *Brighton Tenor Phillips*
Brinell
　　Ex: *Brinell Esther Wilson*
Brinks
　　Ex: *Torina Brinks Fierce*
Briones
　　(BREE-O-NEEZE)
　　Ex: *Felicia Briones Brown*
Brisbane
　　Ex: *Xavier Brisbane Cordovino*
Brisdale
　　Ex: *Sarah Brisdale Phoenix*
Bristol
　　Ex: *Carrie Bristol Wallace*
Briston
　　Ex: *Sylvia Briston Sanders*
Brive
　　Ex: *Randall Brive Welks*
Brix
　　Ex: *Brix Brody*
Brockton
　　Ex: *Raquel Brockton Stone*
Brooklyn
　　Ex: *Cedric Brooklyn Isles*
Brubeck
　　Ex: *Jorin Brubeck Giles*

Bryce
Ex: *Leon Bryce Saber*
Buckeye
Ex: *Buckeye Kirtland*
Buick
Ex: *Roland Buick VanBuhler*
Bulgaria
Ex: *Valin Bulgaria Rix*
Buren
(BJURE-IN)
Ex: *Sibbel Buren Cains*
Burlin
Ex: *Burlin Colton Vandenbosch*
Buruma
Ex: *Buruma Georgiana Calder*
Buzby
Ex: *Buzby Vierra*
Buzz
Ex: *Buzz Sales*
Byer
Ex: *Noland Byer Wright*
Byrd
(BIRD)
Ex: *Byrd Sellice Stare*
Byxbee
Ex: *Byxbee Steeles*

C
>Ex: *C Trenor Cohen*

Caan
>Ex: *Caan Clorox Coleman*

Cabri
>Ex: *Cabri Tiles Walker*

Cache
>Ex: *Cache Steven Walton*

Cactus
>Ex: *Cactus Karen Teales*

Cade
>Ex: *Cade Willis Toland*

Cadell
>Ex: *Cadell Milt Tyland*

Cadet
>Ex: *Cadet Walker Thomas*

Caetano
>(KAY-TA-NO)
>Ex: *Caetano Michelle Torinelli*

Cahlia
>(KA-LEE-A)
>Ex: *Cahlia Nelly Marcello*

Caige
>Ex: *Caige Julan Dorlanski*

Caine
>Ex: *Caine Wexler Krinski*

Cairns
>Ex: *Cairns Mae Kotovsky*

Cairo
>Ex: *Cairo Sin Rallencourt*

Calan
>Ex: *Calan Marcus Christoff*

Calico
>Ex: *Calico Torrie Lowery*

California
>Ex: *California Stevens*

Calin
Ex: *Calin Serin Thomas*
Calista
Ex: *Calista Marie Genetti*
Calistoga
Ex: *Calistoga Henni Stiles*

Calix
Ex: *Calix Jay Imura*
Callia
Ex: *Callia Wexford Ikes*
Calloway
Ex: *Calloway Berin Tales*
Calypso
Ex: *Jorin Calypso Ikeda*
Calyptus
Ex: *Calyptus Connie Hale*
Calyx
Ex: *Calyx Lauren Moreida*
Camden
Ex: *Camden Milen Jones*
Campari
Ex: *Campari Emin Vallenstone*
Canada
Ex: *Canada Lane Montgomery*
Cannon
Ex: *John Cannon Jeffries*
Cano
(KAY-NO)
Ex: *Cano Oscar Morano*
Canoe
Ex: *Canoe Francisco Siquedis*
Canon
Ex: *Canon Lising Gainor*
Cantor
Ex: *Cantor Ibarra Huntington*
Canyon
Ex: *Canyon Sara Harrington*

Caples
> Ex: *Sylvia Caples Price*

Caranda
> Ex: *Caranda Marie Hiranza*

Caravel
> Ex: *Caravel Stevens*

Carib
> Ex: *Carib Bailen Harcourt*

Carline
> Ex: *Carline Carolyn Dvorsky*

Carma
> Ex: *Carma Lynn Dorrentile*

Carmine
> Ex: *Carmine Pritchard*

Carnet
> Ex: *Carnet Rose Osoria*

Carrington
> Ex: *Carrington Steiner Sills*

Carrisa
> Ex: *Carrisa Soreen Duval*

Cartouce
> Ex: *Cartouce Avila Sassano*

Casco
> Ex: *Casco Marin Winfield*

Caselli
> Ex: *Caselli Jane Torrence*

Cashmere
> Ex: *Cashmere Rolls*

Casino
> Ex: *Casino T Wexford*

Cassel
> Ex: *Cassel Leah Ferrington*

Cassia
> Ex: *Cassia Jillan Kales*

Catala
> Ex: *Catala Line Azevedo*

Catalia
>   Ex: *Catalia Loren Illando*

Cavel
>   Ex: *Cavel Whitmore Thomas*

Caven
>   Ex: *Caven Dallen Tares*

Cavon
>   Ex: *Cavon Smiley Spears*

Cayes
>   Ex: *Cayes Smith*

Cayman
>   Ex: *Valerie Cayman Baboolovitch*

Cayne
>   Ex: *Cayne Aylin Seales*

Cea
>   (SAY-UH)
>   Ex: *Cea Miles Chang*

Cedar
>   Ex: *Cedar Ray Chetkovich*

Celadon
>   Ex: *Robert Celandon Eschellman*

Cerro
>   Ex: *Cerro Ethridge Wales*

Cerulean
>   Ex: *Cerulean Palm*

Ceryle
>   (SARE-ULL)
>   Ex: *Ceryle Jane Wexford*

Cessna
>   Ex: *Cessna C Lee*

Ceylon
>   Ex: *Ceylon Iwataki*

Cezanne
>   Ex: Cezanne Cantacello Chagall
>   Ex: *Delano Chagall Writman*

Chaise
>   Ex: *Chaise Alice Dain*

Chanterelle
>Ex: *Chanterelle Marilyn Leonetta*

Chantrey
>Ex: *Chantrey Anne Durantine*

Charlize
>Ex: *Charlize Theron*
>Ex: *Charlize Flores Pope*

Chartreuse
>Ex: *Chartreuse Giovella*

Chase
>Ex: *Chase Perrin Thompson*

Chavall
>Ex: *Lauren Chavall Pritton*

Cheetah
>Ex: *Cheetah Montgomery*

Chelo
>Ex: *Chelo Perrin Payne*

Cheney
>Ex: *Cheney Riles Jorgenson*

Chettah
>Ex: *Chettah Jack*

Chevron
>Ex: *Chevron Jordan Collins*

Cheyenne
>Ex: *Samantha Cheyenne Colanson*

Chianti
>Ex: *Chianti Belle Marlena*

Chiarello
>Ex: *Chiarello Roland Marlentono*

Chime
>Ex: *Chime Susan Paddington*

Chimmney
>Ex: *Chimmney Toland Rhomberg*

Chinex
>Ex: *Chinex T Richardson*

Chiron
>Ex: *Chiron Page Williford*

Chisel
> Ex: *Chisel Stallworth*

Chisholm
> Ex: *Rex Chisholm Weldencour*

Chivallo
> Ex: *Chivallo C Errinson*

Chloe
> Ex: *Chloe David Quinn*

Choco
> Ex: *Choco Rodriguez*

Christele
> Ex: *Christele Marie Korvinovitch*

Chrome
> Ex: *Chrome Baker*

Chrysler
> Ex: *Chrysler T Bookland*

Ciente
> (CEE-EN-TEE)
> Ex: *Ciente Railin Sorentis*

Cinder
> Ex: *Cinder Coland Sandelco*

Cisco
> Ex: *Cisco Bryer Robertson*

Citrus
> Ex: *Citrus Norland Brightenson*

Civa
> Ex: *Civa Paulna Lerrinfjord*

Claesz
> (CLAYS)
> Ex: *Claesz Roland Sankovich*

Claremont
> Ex: *Julie Claremont Reid*

Claret
> Ex: *Claret Virin Colbrin*

Clarinda
> Ex: *Clarinda Vellis Satomi*

Clem
> Ex: *Clem T Marcovich*

Clemence
>Ex: *Clemence Aaron Vallentole*

Cleto
>(CLAY-TOE)
>Ex: *Cleto Peters Stevens*

Clifton
>Ex: *Clifton Jalice Pallerton*

Cline
>Ex: *Cline Waler Hunterton*

Clone
>Ex: *Clone C Pixford*

Clove
>Ex: *Clove Eastons Phillips*

Clydesdale
>Ex: *Julie Clydesdale Walker*

Coad
>Ex: *Coad Maxton Zillman*

Coast
>Ex: *Coast Emily Syers*

Cobalt
>Ex: *Bexler Cobalt Black*

Cochran
>Ex: *Jaron Cochran Sails*

Coda
>Ex: *Coda Stiles*

Codex
>Ex: *Codex Martinoff*

Cohiba
>Ex: *Cohiba Anne Lexington*

Colan
>Ex: *Colan Robert Goldstone*

Colby
>Ex: *Colby Cherin Villentoy*

Cole
>Ex: *Cole Jackson*

Colston
>Ex: *Colston Wexford Appleby*

Colton
> Ex: *Colton Sorenti Carontonella*

Coltrane
> Ex: *Jack Coltrane Sacks*

Colusa
> Ex: *Colusa Rebecca Johnston*

Coney
> Ex: *Coney Marta Gulbrandsen*

Confetti
> Ex: *Confetti Anna Tanson*

Congo
> Ex: *Congo Ryanson*

Conifer
> Ex: *Roland Conifer Walker*

Connecticut
> Ex: *Connecticut Jones*

Connel
> Ex: *Samuel Connel Hatson*

Connolly
> Ex: *Jill Connolly Max*

Conroe
> Ex: *Conroe Marton Smith*

Consuelo
> Ex: *Consuelo Maria Corinna*

Copine
> Ex: *Copine Andrew Bondes*

Coppola
> Ex: *Darwin Coppola Dales*

Coral
> Ex: *Coral Franchesca Mareno*

Corbett
> Ex: *Corbett Baxter Bails*

Cordele
> Ex: *Cordele Rainy Nexford*

Corinthe
> Ex: *Corinthe Anne Phillips*

Corion
> Ex: *Corion Bix Styford*

Corlee
    Ex: *Corlee Laura Lee*
Corlita
    Ex: *Corlita Maria Vinticella*
Corlon
    Ex: *Derrin Colon Giles*
Cornet
    Ex: *Cornet Stevens*

Corniche
    Ex: *Corniche Madella Sarrento*
Corolla
    Ex: *Corolla Seico*
Corona
    Ex: *Stella Corona Stoleno*
Corsair
    Ex: *Corsair Day Ennington*
Corsica
    Ex: *Corsica Jane Sovento*
Corsican
    Ex: *Rex Corsican Sane*
Cortex
    Ex: *Joran Cortex Lexton*
Cortola
    Ex: *Cortola Mae DiCenza*
Cosby
    Ex: *Cosby Daylin Ford*
Cosmo
    Ex: *Cosmo T Worrenton*
Costello
    Ex: *Costello Salino Rivera*
Cove
    Ex: *Cove Waldon*
Covey
    Ex: *Covey C Rains*
Covin
    Ex: *Covin Walker Tapes*

Coy

Ex: *Coy Day Osborne*

Coyle

Ex: *Coyle T Wexler*

Coyote

Ex: *Coyote Phillips*

Crane

Ex: *Jacqueline Crane Sarringston*

Creole

Ex: *Creole Batchelor Scott*

Crimson

Ex: *Crimson Berrin Sills*

Curry

Ex: *Curry Amy Millen*

Cristalle

Ex: *Cristalle Rose Hyzer*

Crivello

Ex: *Crivello Black Domingo*

Crosby

Ex: *Crosby Ashford Jakes*

Curran

Ex: *Curran Rose Isquierda*

Cutter

Ex: *Cutter Thompson Tyes*

Cyan

(SIGH-ANN)

Ex: *Cyan Jack Jones*

Cyber

Ex: *Cyber J Cain*

Cyrano

Ex: *Cyrano T Wintercole*

Cyrene

Ex: *Cyrene Tara Smith*

Cysco

Ex: *Cysco Vallens Enjala*

D
> Ex: *D Terrin Silton*

D.C.
> Ex: *D.C. Lou Tarton*

Dagger
> Ex: *Dagger Q Maxton*

Dagget
> Ex: *Dagget Steener Thomas*

Dailin
> Ex: *Dailin Extin Roebin*

Dako
> Ex: *Dako Bitto Tykes*

Dakota
> Ex: *Dakota Tonin Riter*

Dalea
> (DAY-LEE-UH)
> Ex: *Daylea Raykin Santos*

Dali
> (DOLLY)
> Ex: *Dali Catalin Pellor*

Dane
> Ex: *Dane Wilton Pile*

Danko
> Ex: *Danko Cains*

Danridge
> Ex: *Danridge Wilson Merikan*

Dash
> Ex: *Dash Errand*

Dashwood
> Ex: *Dashwood Willis Tones*

Davia
> Ex: *Davia Bassil Fillant*

Davos
> (DAYVOS or DAH-VOS)
> Ex: *Jallin Davos Smith*

Dayouai
> (DAY-OO-I)
> Ex: *Dayouai Jane Corstan*

Dax
> Ex: *Dax Cherrin Walker*

Dayao
> (DAY-O)
> Ex: *Dayao Salin More*

Daytona
> Ex: *Daytona Jail Corsithe*

Deakin
> Ex: *Deakin Jones*

Decca
> Ex: *Decca Sarah Smokes*

Decco
> Ex: *Decco Day Blige*

December
> Ex: *December Staples*

Deiniol
> (DAY-IN-EE-OL)
> Ex: *Deiniol Cartoon Songsworth*

Deisel
> Ex: *Deisel Cross*

Dela
> (DAY-LA)
> Ex: *Sophia Dela Costa*

Delaine
> Ex: *Delaine Silton Miles*

Delana
> (DA-LAY-NA)
> Ex: *Delana Rae Cartwright*

Delaney
> Ex: *Delaney Sints Topelin*

Delano
> Ex: *Delano Corrin Stevens*

Delft
> Ex: *Delft Roybin Fents*

Delia
    Ex: *Delia Sarts Ritz*
Delirium
    Ex: *Delirium Jippes*
Delmar
    Ex: *Delmar Berrin Tye*
Delox
    Ex: *Delox Boxer Boyle*
Delphine
    Ex: *Vena Delphine Aints*
Delphinium
    Ex: *Suzanne Delphinium Wirn*
Delray
    Ex: *Delray Walker*
Delta
    Ex: *Delta Sebrin Fikes*
Deluna
    Ex: *Juliana Deluna Korinski*
Deluxe
    Ex: *Deluxe Fins*
Delwood
    Ex: *Max Delwood Beens*
Denio
    Ex: *Denio Bye Cortes*
Dennett
    Ex: *Dennett Bilston Blike*
Denslowe
    Ex: *Stuart Denslowe Giles*
Denver
    Ex: *Denver Jana Jefferson*
Derby
    Ex: *Porche Derby Emerson*
Dermit
    Ex: *Dermit Townsend*
Dero
    Ex: *Zachery Dero Sorringson*

Derringer
  Ex: *Zoe Derringer Whites*
Desert
  Ex: *Susie Desert Rain*
Desoto
  Ex: *Desoto Baxter Nells*
Detoro
  Ex: *Detoro Bolts Black*
Detroit
  Ex: *Detroit Stevens*

Deuce
  Ex: *Deuce Kix*
Devons
  Ex: *Devons Chester Malone*
Dice
  Ex: *Dice Bricks*
Dideon
  Ex: *Dideon Jacobs*
Diehl
  (DEAL)
  Ex: *Diehl Dalila Doll*
Diem
  Ex: *Diem Gordon Charts*
Dieval
  (DEE-VULL)
  Ex: *Rochele Dieval Morgan*
Digit
  Ex: *Digit Cato Richmond*
Dine
  Ex: *Dine Erriks Dates*
Dingo
  Ex: *Dingo Datsun*
Dino
  Ex: *Dino Fornelli Salerno*
Dira
  Ex: *Dira Siya Sanes*

Discin
> Ex: *Discin Satcliff*

Disco
> Ex: *Disco Bixler Wayne*

Disney
> Ex: *Disney Jane Carrington*

Dita
> Ex: *Dita Rose*

Ditto
> Ex: *Ditto Ray Johnson*

Divine
> Ex: *Jill Divine Black*

Dizzy
> Ex: *Dizzy Wexler Phillips*

Djourne
> Ex: *Djourne Sintro Sails*

Docena
> Ex: *Docena Marie Corlando*

Dohn
> (DOAN)
> *Dohn Jakes*

Doll
> Ex: *Doll Gypsie Wakes*

Dolland
> Ex: *Dolland Basco Wrights*

Dominica
> Ex: *Dominica Rae Costillo*

Domino
> Ex: *Domino Factor Price*

Donegan
> Ex: *Donegan Bailey McKinnon*

Donner
> Ex: *Sylvia Donner Rhodes*

Dorado
> Ex: *Dorado Rachel Alexis*

Doric
> Ex: *Doric Rick Ales*

Dory
>   Ex: *Dory Chitin Sales*

Dox
>   Ex: *Dox Walker*

Doyle
>   Ex: *Doyle Jenner Tomms*

Drago
>   Ex: *Drago Cranston Sikes*

Dresden
>   Ex: *Dresden Saron Timton*

Drexel
>   Ex: *Drexel Lurey Finns*

Driscoll
>   Ex: *Driscoll Stevens*

Dryden
>   Ex: *Dryden Dailin Bronks*

Dubbs
>   Ex: *Ryan Dubbs Dyne*

Dumosa
>   Ex: *Dumosa Tina Kintall*

Dundes
>   Ex: *Dundes John Stone*

Dune
>   Ex: *Dune Rakin Cranes*

Dupont
>   Ex: *Dupont Brighton Price*

Durango
>   Ex: *Durango Langston Plains*

Durham
>   Ex: *Durham Berrin Black*

Duvall
>   Ex: *Joseph Duvall Modello*

Duveen
>   Ex: *Duveen Jensen*

E
    Ex: *E Landor Erill*
Eames
    Ex: *Eames Peerson*
Early
    Ex: *Early Cheeks*
Easson
    (EE-SON)
    Ex: *Easson Tiner Take*
East
    Ex: *East Base Texlyn*
Easton
    Ex: *Easton Wakes*
Eaton
    Ex: *Eaton John Wallace*
Eves
    Eves Bain Casssil
Ebbet
    Ex: *Ebbet Brubeck Caid*
Echto
    Ex: *Echto Zydo Core*
Edenton
    Ex: *Edenton Whisko Fent*
Edsel
    Ex: *Edsel Bryerson Akhotani*
Egypt
    Ex: *Lauren Egypt Paikes*
Eich
    Ex: *Eich Rin Weyton*
Eiffel
    (EYE-FILL)
    Ex: *Sara Eiffel Davis*
Elecka
    Ex: *Elecka Raine*
Electra
    Ex: *Electra Bates*

Eleno
> (EL-AY-NO)
> Ex: *Eleno Cortex*

Elgin
> Ex: *Lorissa Elgin Cycourt*

Elk
> Ex: *Elk Dindo Brooks*

Elkus
> Ex: *Elkus Finns*

Elle
> Ex: *Elle Sarta*

Ellington
> Ex: *Jake Ellington Paston*

Elmont
> Ex: *Elmont Kingston*

Elmwood
> Ex: *Elmwood Riles*

Ember
> Ex: *Susan Ember Brakeston*

Emileen
> Ex: *Emileen Sue Pritchford*

Emmet
> Ex: *Emmet Phillip Lynch*

Encino
> Ex: *Encino Straws*

Enez
> (EE-NEZ)
> Ex: *Enez Pixton Drake*

Enos
> (EE-NOS)
> Ex: *Enos Sartin Tale*

Ensley
> Ex: *Jill Ensley Winter*

Eola
> (EE-O-LA)
> Ex: *Eola Wikes*

Eoline
>Ex: *Sally Eoline Baker*

Ephraim
>Ex: *Ephraim Sayad*

Erasmus
>Ex: *Erasmus Clones*

Erte
>Ex: *Melissa Erte Cannes*

Escalon
>Ex: *Escalon Cayanos Seville*

Escondido
>Ex: *Escondido Jay*

Escovedo
>Ex: *Escovedo Valdine Ramiriz*

Esenel
>Ex: *Esenel Beckler Highland*

Essena
>Ex: *Essena Williams Sen*

Esseno
>(ESS-EE-NO)
>Ex: *Esseno Serrina Haywood*

Estero
>Ex: *Estero Grant Lorrento*

Etzel
>Ex: *Hillary Etzel Hayes*

Eubie
>(U-BEE)
>Ex: *Eubie Reeds*

Euclid
>Ex: *Euclid Cintra Sashton*

Euenar
>(YOU-N-R)
>Ex: *Euenar Petrash*

Eulalia
>(OO-LAY-LEE-AH)
>Ex: *Eulalia Carey*

Evora
>(EV-OR-AH or EE-VOR-AH)
>Ex: *Evora Marie Genetti Bautista*

Fax
>Ex: *Fax Carrington*

Fellini
>Ex: *Base Fellini Jackonetti*

Fenton
>Ex: *Fenton Keller*

Fidelma
>Ex: *Fidelma May*

Fidora
>Ex: *Fidora Stallone*

Filbert
>Ex: *Filbert Paston*

Fillmore
>Ex: *Amy Fillmore Bransford*

Filly
>Ex: *Filly Wheaton Sulikowski*

Fimo
>Ex: *Fimo Raites*

Finley
>Ex: *Finley Sarah Smith*

Finnial
>Ex: *Jacqueline Finnial Sanns*

Fire
>Ex: *Fire Richo Roberts*

Fisbie
>Ex: *Fisbie Jill Anniston*

Fisher
>Ex: *Fisher Kayler Brown*

Flash
>Ex: *Flash Phelps*

Flicka
>Ex: *Flicka Alexa Peralta Maria McGurrin*

Flinn
>Ex: *Flinn Martine Perrinson*

Flint
>Ex: *Flint Fredricks*

Flip
>Ex: *Flip Johnson Jones*

Florinda
>Ex: *Florinda Maria Corrina Fuentes*

Flynt
>Ex: *Flynt Axton*

Foley
>Ex: *Foley Maxton Freeland*

Folsom
>Ex: *Folsom Baker Howes*

Fontana
>Ex: *Fontana Greene*

Formica
>Ex: *Formica Dinette*

Forsythe
>Ex: *Carlson Forsythe Santini*

Fossil
>Ex: *Jackson Fossil Dred*

Froujke
>(FROWK)
>Ex: *Melissa Froujke Abbott*

Fulton
>Ex: *Sara Fulton Mendelcraton*

Gadget
    Ex: *Michael Gadget David*
Gaenor
    Ex: *Gaenor Wake Merrins*
Galena
    Ex: *Galena Carlotta Sorento*
Gannett
    Ex: *Jerrund Gannett Torrintale*
Gaton
    Ex: *Gaton Barry Trikes*
Gaugin
    Ex: *Texler Gaugin Stevens*
Gavlin
    Ex: *Gavlin Martin Sperry*
Geary
    Ex: *Geary Walton Goldstine*
Gekko

    Ex: *Gekko Brakes*
Geneva
    Ex: *Geneva Betty Riche*
Geo
    Ex: *Geo Jorland Giles*
Gero
    (JARE-O)
    Ex: *Gero Martinez Blake*
Gershwin
    Ex: *Gershwin Batin Moore*
Gimo
    Ex: *Gimo Perrini*
Gin
    Ex: *Gin Thomas*
Ginseng
    Ex: *Ginseng Sara Ellsworth*
Godiva
    Ex: *Godiva Bright*
Gold
    Ex: *Jack Gold Rain*

Goleta
>Ex: *Cindy Goleta Tinstow*

Gotham
>Ex: *Gotham Mary Erikson*

Grain
>Ex: *Grain Bill Miles*

Grandcanyon
>Ex: *Lucille Grandcanyon Porter*

Green
>Ex: *Green Teakes*

Grenada
>Ex: *Grenada Prascilla Cortnella*

Griffin
>Ex: *Griffin Sikes*

Grinnel
>Ex: *Sylvia Grinnel Marin*

Guage
>Ex: *Guage Willis Rhork*

Guatemala
>Ex: *Sussana Guatemala Cerres*

Guaymas
>Ex: *Guaymas Ellen Winston*

Guilder
>Ex: *Guilder Lane Rhodes*

Guilin
>Ex: *Guilin Saxby Price*

Gunn
>Ex: *Gunn Lewis Steer*

Haasel
>(HA-SULL)
>
>Ex: *Haasel Jordan Paytes*

Hale
>Ex: *J Hale Jones*

Halifax
>Ex: *Samuel Halifax Baxter*

Halloway
>Ex: *Halloway Cobalt Shores*

Halogen
>Ex: *Halogen Lindsey Sands*

Halon
>Ex: *Halon Gregory Rings*

Hajin
>Ex: *Hajin Rites*

Hanover
>Ex: *Manny Hanover Rubenstein*

Harlem
>Ex: *Harlem Lucy Strikes*

Harmon
>Ex: *Harmon Lenny Sills*

Haromi
>(HARE-O-ME)
>
>Ex: *Marissa Haromi Jentzen*

Harrell
>Ex: *Harrell Roland Rey*

Harumi
>(HA-ROO-ME)
>
>Ex: *Jules Harumi Johnston*

Harvard
>Ex: *Harvard Stone*

Havana
>Ex: *Havana Marie Sartaynja*

Hayden
>Ex: *Hayden Coulter Dougherty*

Hayes
>Ex: *Hayes Brinell Sares*

Haylo
>Ex: *Felicia Haylo Vintercourt*

Hayworth
>Ex: *Hayworth Rachel Llord*

Hazelton
>Ex: *Perry Hazelton Phillips*

Hazen
>Ex: *Hazen Jacqueline Saints*

Hemlock
>Ex: *Clorissa Hemlock Rands*

Hennesey
>Ex: *Hennesey C White*

Hepsebaugh
>Ex: *Hepsebaugh Harlan Spivey*

Heron
>Ex: *Heron Aston Kales*

Heusen
>Ex: *Robert Heusen Storlan*

Hiero
>(HE-AIR-OH)
>Ex: *Jacques Hiero Linnson*

Highland
>Ex: *Bobby Highland Black*

Hiko
>(HE-KO)
>Ex: *Hiko Ditto Dayes*

Hilo
>Ex: *Hilo Bento Takano*

Hilton
>Ex: *Hilton James Heuer*

Hemmingway
>Ex: *Eldridge Hemmingway
>Ryemore*

Hine
>Ex: *Hine Lester Loomis*

Hockney
>Ex: *Gerrund Hockney Jones*

Hollywood
>   Ex: *Hollywood Sam Stelleri*

Hopkins
>   Ex: *Hopkins Toland Dex*

Howlin
>   Ex: *Perrin Howlin Lanlon*

Huxley
>   Ex: *Huxley Tennor Rainnin*

Hyatt
>   Ex: *Hyatt Latton Drake*

Hyde
>   Ex: *Hyde Willis Laton*

Hydro
>   Ex: *Hydro Piedmont Pakes*

I
>   Ex: *I Corlin Tynan*

Iaco
>   (EE-AH-KO)
>   Ex: *Iaco Green Satayno*

Iakora
>   (EE-AH-KOR-AH)
>   Ex: *Iakora Lynn Korani*

Ichino
>   (IH-KEY-NO)
>   Ex: *Ichino Moro Kobin*

Idol
>   Ex: *Idol West*

Idoya
>   (EE-DOY-UH)
>   Ex: *Idoya Corrine Bess*

Iko
>   (EE-KO)
>   Ex: *Iko Theresa Norkandinsko*

Ilex
>   Ex: *Ilex Black*

Illa
>   Ex: *Illa Vicenza Sorrena*

Illinois
>   Ex: *Illinois Stevens*

Imo
>   Ex: *Imo Ricks*

Imogen
>   Ex: *Julyn Imogen Kate*

Impala
>   Ex: *Roquel Imapala Moore*

Inc
>   Ex: *Inc Sands*

Indiana
>   Ex: *Indiana Tappin Roads*

Indigo
>   Ex: *Indigo Jane Wethers*

Indio
Ex: *Indio Salentino*
Indo
Ex: *Indo Lowpin Becks*
Indra
Ex: *Sara Indra Fines*
Inglewood
Ex: *Inglewood Baxter Weslyn*
Ingo
Ex: *Ingo Rice*
Iolo
Ex: *Iolo Charlin Torrine*
Iona
Ex: *Iona Phillips*
Ionica
Ex: *Ionica Vaness Dietz*
Iora
(EE-OR-UH)
Ex: *Iora Rainey Mae*
Iota
Ex: *David Iota Juleston*
Iowa
Ex: *Jennifer Iowa Banks*

Ipso
Ex: *Ipso Noland Dorkanski*
Ireland
Ex: *Chet Ireland Chase*
Iro
Ex: *Sperry Iro Packard*
Irvine
Ex: *Jaqueline Irvine West*
Ishin
Ex: *Sidney Ishin Lee*
Isiolo
(I-CEE-O-LOW)
Ex: *Isiolo Kay Tano*

Island

    Ex: *Jenny Island Saints*

Isle

    Ex: *John Isle Rainin*

Isola

    Ex: *Isola Crae*

Ives

    Ex: *Bateman Ives Lyndenson*

Ivory

    Ex: *Jorlin Ivory Cates*

Izzy

    Ex: *Izzy Fenns*

Jaakko
> (JAY-KO)
> Ex: *Jaakko C Rappaport*

Jacaro
> Ex: *Jacaro J London*

Jaeger
> (YEA-GER)
> Ex: *Jaeger T Ollander*

Jag
> Ex: *Jag J Tekkor*

Jaice
> Ex: *Jaice Stevens*

Jakarta
> Ex: *Jakarta Black*

Jalon
> Ex: *Jalon Perry Smith*

Jamaica
> Ex: *Jamaica Earl Jones*

Jamal
> Ex: *Jamal Even Saintes*

Janneau
> (JAN-O)
> Ex: *Julie Janneau West*

Javanese
> Ex: *Javanese Ojeda*

Jayena
> Ex: *Ruby Jaena Bates*

Jayenel
> Ex: *Jayenel C Rollins*

Jenkins
> Ex: *Jenkins Steele*

Jergen
> Ex: *Jergen Aston Borrenskovitch*

Jerico
> Ex: *Jerico Jaime Sorrenton*

Jerilyn
> Ex: *Jerilyn B Maxton*

Jersey
> Ex: *Jersey Shores*

Jetson
> Ex: *Jetson Khorin Dodson*

Jetta
> Ex: *Jetta Leslie Gonsalez*

Jetty
> Ex: *Jetty Krausen*

Jeust
> Ex: *Jeust Morena*

Jhumpa
> (JOOM-PA)
> Ex: *Jhumpa Lahiri*

Jimno
> Ex: *Jimno Montgomery*

Jinx
> *Jinx Carmen Corona*

Jitzu
> Ex: *Jitzu Imura Icardo*

Jixi
> Ex: *Jixi Marshine*

Jovan
> (YO-VAUGHN)
> Ex: *Jovan Satner Solkantovich*

Josefa
> Ex: *Josefa Farine Tulare*

Jucara
> Ex: *Jucara Victor Monrovio*

Juneau
> Ex: *Juneau Sarmiento Rontino*

Jungle
> Ex: *Sumara Jungle Mirantes*

Juniper
> Ex: *Juniper Jade Rellina*

Justice
> Ex: *Milton Justice Sadler*

Jute
> Ex: *Jute Clifford McCutcheon*

Kaanapali
    Ex: *Kaanapali Lea Loa*
Kahlo
    Ex: *Kahlo Dalo McCrea*
Kaiser
    Ex: *Kaiser McDonald*
Kalana
    Ex: *Kalana Rena Ferrara*
Kale
    Ex: *Kale T Wexford*
Kandinsky
    Ex: *Rich Kandinsky Fischman*
Kane
    Ex: *Kane Angela Ferrintino*
Kansas
    Ex: *Kansas Cantor Fikes*
Karastan
    Ex: *Karastan Roselyn Golde*
Kardel
    Ex: *Kardel Griffen Jefferson*
Karim
    Ex: *Salana Karim Jutowski*
Kavel
    Ex: *Kavel Arron Kirtland*
Kayak
    Ex: *Kayak Kristin Klassen*
Kayhan
    Ex: *Kayhan Ghodsi*
Keemun
    Ex: *Keemun Cane Sasnish*
Keena
    Ex: *Keena Teresa McKinley*
Kegan
    Ex: *Kegan McDougald*
Keiko
    (KAY-KO)
    Ex: *Keiko Jul Skate*

Kellog
    Ex: *Kellog Roger Coates*
Kellyn
    Ex: *Kellyn Besty Rhodin*
Kelso
    Ex: *Kelso Ashton Price*
Kendall
    Ex: *Kendall Jay Bexler*
Kendra
    Ex: *Kendra Hanna Smith*
Keno
    Ex: *Keno Jack Sultanin*
Kenova
    Ex: *Kenova Reena Tales*
Kenyon
    Ex: *Kenyon Rales*
Keoka
    Ex: *Keoka Sato Argabright*
Keoki
    Ex: *Keoki C Terrako*
Keoko
    Ex: *Keoko Michelle Catterson*
Kerouac
    Ex: *Kerouac Alderman*
Kestrel
    Ex: *Meagan Kestrel Bharnes*
Keswick
    Ex: *Keswick J Satchfeld*
Kevlin
    Ex: *Kevlin Mars*
Kiliminjaro
    Ex: *Chistopher Kiliminjaro Jonns*
Kilo
    Ex: *Kilo Venlin*
Kilty
    Ex: *Samson Kilty Kales*

Kincaid
 Ex: *Kincaid Rhode*
Kingston
 Ex: *Gerome Kingston Nicholes*
Kiosk
 Ex; Kiosk Banes
Kiowa
 Ex: *Kiowa Bonnie Bates*
Kirala
 Ex: *Kirala Jane Roberts*
Kirin
 Ex: *Kirin Decca Brades*
Kitano
 Ex: *Kitano Wattes*
Klee
 Ex: *Klee Whitten Dorrin*
Knight
 Ex: *Knight Reed*
Knota
 (NOTE-UH)
 Ex: *Knota Steel Rites*
Knox
 Ex: *Wilson Knox Bailerton*
Koala
 Ex: *Koala Richtes*
Kobe
 Ex: *Kobe Lei Pare*
Kodiak
 Ex: *Kodiak Bankington*

Kohler
 Ex: *Kohler C Winston*
Kojak
 Ex: *Kojak Jerrund Morrris*
Kona
 Ex: *Kona Liani Layna*
Koria
 Ex: *Koria Lassin*

Kyburz
    Ex: *Kyburz Teakin Rast*

La Paz
>Ex: *La Paz Holland*

Laakin
>(LA-KIN)
>Ex: *Laakin Jarra Lincot*

Lafayette
>Ex: *Layfayette Lewis*

Lahiri
>Ex: *Lahiri Bareen*

Landon
>Ex: *Landon Cellucci-Maddox*

Lapis
>Ex: *Lapis Jace Stol*

Laredo
>Ex: *John Laredo Settby*

Lariat
>Ex: *Lariat William Finee*

Larissa
>Ex: *Larissa Langston Farr*

Larkin
>Ex: *Larkin Pratmore*

Larkspur
>Ex: *Larkspur Cheryl Rites*

Lasher
>Ex: *Lasher Marx*

Lassen
>Ex: *Lassen C Courts*

Latch
>Ex: *Latch Polin*

Lausanne
>Ex: *Lausanne Sorenna*

Lavell
>Ex: *Lavell Lakeston*

Lawton
>Ex: *Lawton John Coneston*

Laykin
Ex: *Laykin Khares*
Lela
Ex: *Lelongoa Alexa Levi*
Lennox
Ex: *Lisa Lennox Grace*
Leota
Ex: *Leota Jale Scorson*
Levon
Ex: *Levon Miles*
Lexine
Ex: *Lixine Milly Landon*
Lilac
Ex: *Lilac Mazy Moss*
Linc
Ex: *Linc Morgan*
Linden
Ex: *Linden P Argyle*
Lindo
Ex: *Lindo Rondelli*
Linfield
Ex: *Linfield Lawson*
Linnet
Ex: *Torrin Linnet Taylin*
Linwood
Ex: *Linwood Rocksford*
Lirion
Ex: *Jules Lirion Jacket*
Lirium
Ex: *Lirium Nestle*
Lixi
Ex: *Lixi Dobri*
Lodi
(LOW-DYE)
Ex: *Lodi Walker*
London
Ex: *Lauren London Waytes*

Lortel
    Ex: *Lortel Dorensko*
Lotus
    Ex: *Lotus Lee Paxford*
Lovejoy
    Ex: *Julia Lovejoy Sibbet*
Lowell
    Ex: *Lowell Dorin Toland*
Loyola
    Ex: *Loyola Sills Westford*
Lozanos
    Ex: *Lozanos Corone Sabin*
Lucerne
    Ex: *Lucerne T Rexor*
Lucia
    Ex: *Lucia Marie Ginetti*
Luminere
    Ex: *Noreen Luminere Billing*
Lupine
    Ex: *Michael Lupine Blades*
Luxe
    Ex: *Luxe Bocarski*
Lynden
    Ex: *Lynden Stiles*
Lyndon
    Ex: *Lydon Paris*
Lyne
    Ex: *Lyne Marcus Rand*
Lynford
    Ex: *Lynford Price*
Lynon
    Ex: *Lynon Karen Tones*

Lynx
    Ex: *Lynx Setlin*
Lyra
    Ex: *Lyra Karmine*

Masai

   (MA-SIGH)

   Ex: *Masai C Catttamar*

Macado

   Ex: *Macado Crae*

Macay

   Ex: *Macay Foster*

Madeira

   Ex: *Luchesa Madeira Ronneta*

Maddox

   Ex: *Maddox Jolie*

Madras

   Ex: *Jacqueline Madras Bellingcourt*

Madrid

   Ex: *Madrid Sienna Sakes*

Maduro

   Ex: *Julian Maduro Grants*

Magenta

   Ex: *Magenta Rose*

Magnet

   Ex: *Doris Magnet Starlin*

Magnolia

   Ex: *Magnolia Lucy Marrington*

Maiko

   Ex: *Maiko Connor Stennmar*

Maine

   Ex: *Maine Jenner Straits*

Mairobi

   Ex: *Jules Mairobi Braxtin*

Majave

   (MA-YA-VEE)

   Ex: Ex: *Majave Rachel Banes*

Maki

   (MA-KEY)

   Ex: *Maki West Tobenta*

Malachite
Ex: *Malachite Hale*
Malaza
Ex: *Rolin Malaza Spade*
Malden
Ex: *Malden Dean Sonderville*
Maletti
Ex: *Susan Maletti Barrett*
Mallorca
(MY-OR-CA)
Ex: *Mallorca Maria Vanettto*
Malone
Ex: *Malone Stevens*
Malta
Ex: *Malta C Corlanetti*
Mandarin
Ex: *Corinna Mandarin DuPont*
Manet
(MAA-NAY)
Ex: *Senna Manet Pascal*
Mannequin
Ex: *Mannequin Price*
Manx
Ex: *Benjamin Manx Dolland*
Marden
Ex: *Marden Cannor Tillmans*
Marengo
Ex: *Marengo Colant Seremo*
Margolin
Ex: *Margolin Ballantynne*
Marigolde
Ex: *Marigolde Delgado*
Marijke
(MARE-I-KA)
Ex: *Marijke Terpstra*
Marimba
Ex: *Susanne Marimba Felice*

Marina
> Ex: *Marina Rachelle Delano*

Mariner
> Ex: *Islo Mariner Esposito*

Mariposa
> Ex: *Mariposa Leah Freedlund*

Marisol
> Ex: *Marisol Julis Gantt*

Marlin
> Ex: *Marlin Garcia Goldstein*

Marlon
> Ex: *Marlon Henrik Cartsworth*

Marmac
> Ex: *Marmac Jackson Cates*

Maronnet
> Ex: *Marronet Hayden*

Marsala
> Ex: *Marsala Hatheway*

Martell
> Ex: *Martell T Sicado*

Martini
> Ex: *Martini West*

Marwan
> Ex: *Marwan Noel Sabbagh*

Mash
> Ex: *Wexford Mash Trains*

Masonic
> Ex: *Masonic Post*

Match
> Ex: *Match T Mason*

Mateo
> Ex: *Mateo Sortinella*

Matisse
> Ex: *Matisse Berrin Jenni*

Maytag
> Ex: *Maytag Corin Blue*

McAllister
>Ex: *McAllister Payne Webster*

McBey
>Ex: *McBey Darwin Woods*

McCall
>Ex: *McCall Torrence Willks*

McGraw
>Ex: *McGraw Heath*

McGurrin
>Ex: *McGurrin Seton Leibert*

McRae
>Ex: *McRae Ashlin Stockard*

Mecca
>Ex: *Mecca Miles Price*

Medanos
>Ex: *Rachel Medanos Mendoza*

Medina
>Ex: *Medina Ray Rolands*

Meighan
>(MEE-IN)
>Ex: *Meighan Williams Leibert*

Melbourne
>Ex: *Luci Melbourne Arrows*

Melton
>Ex: *Melton Davis*

Memphis
>Ex: *Itore Memphis Sottsass*

Menakhaya
>(MEN-UH-KIE-UH)
>Ex: *Kenna Menakhaya Raines*

Mendel
>Ex: *Mendel Jackson*

Mendocino
>Ex: *Mendocino Parker*

Mercury
>Ex: *Roland Mercury Rohe*

Merdoc
>Ex: *Merdoc Jeffery Payne*

Meridien
>Ex: *Meridien Tamara Grove*

Merino
>Ex: *Merino T Venturo*

Mero
>(MARE-O)
>Ex: *Mero Siquedo Dungala*

Merrimac
>Ex: *Merrimac Scherer*

Mesa
>Ex: *Mesa Zona*

Metro
>Ex: *Metro Baxter*

Mexico
>Ex: *Mexico Santo Viera*

Michigan
>Ex: *David Michigan Lockwood*

Mieno
>(ME-AY-NO)
>Ex: *Mieno Kay Tokin*

Miilo
>(MY-LOW)
>Ex: *Miilo Roberts*

Mikado
>(ME-KA-DO)
>Ex: *Mikado Yoshi Corolla*

Mikkelson
>Ex: *Jack Mikkelson Dice*

Millenium
>Ex: *Maron Millenium Mitchells*

Million
>Ex: *Million Stolinovitchcoff*

Mimosa
>Ex: *Mimosa Maria Martell*

Minda
> Ex: *Minda McDaniels*

Ming
> Ex: *Julie Ming Schwarts*

Mingo
> Ex: *Mingo Nakano*

Minnow
> Ex: *Minnow Parkington*

Minorca
> Ex: *Minorca Ruby*

Minta
> Ex: *Minta Manx*

Minthe
> Ex: *Minthe Alice Dine*

Mirada
> Ex: *Mirada Ferrari*

Mirinda
> Ex: *Mirinda Costa Mira*

Miro
> (MERE-OH)
> Ex: *Nichol Miro Gianni*

Missoula
> Ex: *Missoula Roquelle Montana*

Missouri
> Ex: *Braemar Missouri Jacobs*

Miyako
> Ex: *Miyako Kaytano*

Mizner
> Ex: *Mizner Ritchell Jones*

Mobil
> Ex: *Mobil SonderOrtinez*

Mobile
> Ex: *Mobile Sari Osmani*

Mobius
> Ex: *Mobius Kates*

Modena
Ex: *Modena Ayla Sorrento*
Mojave
Ex: *Kaydo Mojave Brit*
Molina
Ex: *Molina Maria Maretti*
Monaco
Ex: *Monaco Angela Mida*
Monet
(MO-NAY)
Ex: *Monet Jina Latin*
Money
Ex: *Jackson Money Takks*
Monopole
Ex: *Reann Monopole Burlynn*
Monroe
Ex: *Monroe Stennson*
Montague
(MON-TA-GIEW)
Ex: *Montague Jase*
Montana
Ex: *Montana Jameson Larussa*
Montego
Ex: *Lawernce Montego Venetto*
Montgomery
Ex: *Eldon Montgomery Blues*
Montrose
Ex: *Montrose West*
Moreno
Ex: *Serrin Moreno Caines*
Morro
Ex: *Constance Morro Lattin*
Mortise
Ex: *Mortise Laskin Fornello*
Mosaic
Ex: *Mosaic T Osorino*

Moscow
>Ex: *Lorraine Moscow Antonia*

Mosson
>(MO-SON)
>Ex: *Mosson Tory Martinez*

Mota
>(MO-TAH)
>Ex: *Mota James*

Moxie
>Ex: *Moxie Perrin Miotel*

Muana Loa
>Ex: *Muana Loa Iles*

Muller
>(MIU-LER)
>Ex: *Muller Giordan Rebbel*

Mvolo
>Ex: *Mvolo Rex Rientos*

Myo
>Ex: *Myo Goldstein*

Myorca
>Ex: *Myorca Yoskiko Tallavera*

Myrh
>(MURR)
>Ex: *Dusty Myrh Blone*

Nashville
    Ex: *Susan Nashville Hartlin*
Namerology
    Ex: *Namerology Praxton Price*
Nandina
    Ex: *Nandina T Sparks*
Nanimo
    Ex: *Nanimo Pettiman*
Narsai
    (NAR-CEE)
    Narsai Michael David
Nari
    Ex: *Michelle Nari Abbott*
Nasa
    Ex: *Nasa Warren Tackin*
Nash
    Ex: *Nash Wailin Greenes*
Nashville
    Ex: *Nashville Cats*
Nato
    Ex: *Nato Sorren Grove*
Natoma
    Ex: *Natoma Rocken State*
Nautica
    Ex: *Sally Nautica Holland*
Navak
    Ex: *Navak Pond*
Navy
    Ex: *Navy Connor Jannets*
Neo
    Ex: *Neo Macintosh*
Neon
    Ex: *Neon Charles Whitfield*
Neptune
    Ex: *Celestine Neptune Sands*
Nero
    Ex: *Nero Graham*

Nether
>   Ex: *Nether Hollander*

Nevin
>   Ex: *Nivin Place*

Newport
>   Ex: *Newport Seymore Glickstein*

Nico
>   Ex: *Nico Cartwright*

Nido
>   Ex: *Nido Dakin Rappacourt*

Nightingale
>   Ex: *Nightingale Deena Agellin*

Nikel
>   Ex: *Nikel Blanes*

Nile
>   Ex: *Nile Steve Witherton*

Niro
>   Ex: *Niro Stone*

Nitro
>   Ex: *Nitro Glass Storler*

Nonce
>   Ex: *Nonce Pera Valdeen*

Norrell
>   Ex: *Maureen Norrell Blackes*

Noveau
>   (NO-VO)
>   Ex: *Noveau Charlin Nemin*

Novena
>   (NO-VEH-NUH or NO-VEE-NA)
>   Ex: *Novena Mari Solento*

O
Ex: *O Rona Coran*
Obit
Ex: *Obit T Jones*
Odeon
Ex: *Odeon Ryan Wilson*
Odessa
Ex: *Odessa Jana Erikson*
Odin
Ex: *Odin C Tollin*
Oeno
(O-AY-NO)
Ex: *Oeno Kaylin Lewis*
Ohana
Ex: *Ohana Bixland*
Ohai
(O-HIGH)
Ex: *Ohai Matson*
Ohio
Ex: *Ohio Barrents*
Oka
Ex: *Oka Shares*
O'keefe
Ex: *O'keefe Perrins Stonnings*
Ola
Ex: *Ola Ferrindo*
Olin
Ex: *Olin C Ferrari*
Olinda
Ex: *Olinda Dashmar*
Olive
Ex: *Olive Terrin Boyanowski*
Omaha
Ex: *Omaha Makler Brinnelsson*
Oman
Ex: *Oman Wastin Carrington*

Omega
> Ex: *Omega Benin Garristore*

Omer
> Ex: *Omer Clayes Fellinton*

Ooloo
> (EW-LOO)
> Ex: *Ooloo Emily Waldron*

Opal
> Ex: *Opal Sella Hendrickson*

Oram
> Ex: *Oram Pine Clares*

Orbit
> Ex: *Orbit Stells*

Orchid
> Ex: *Rainey Orchid Dyne*

Oreana
> (O-REE-NA)
> Ex: *Oreana Annie Bates*

Orilla
> Ex: *Orilla Linda Vienos*

Orinda
> Ex: *Orinda Day Ilanda*

Oriole
> Ex: *Oriole Stevens*

Orion
> Ex: *Orion Bateson*

Oro
> Ex: *Oro C Mendelsen*

Orrin
> Ex: *Orrin Craston Flips*

Orsi
> Ex: *Franklin Orsi Lauder*

Ortez
> Ex: *Ortez Manuel Carracas*

Orvieto
> Ex: *Orvieto Jones*

Orwell
    Ex: *Orwell Briscoe*
Osaka
    Ex: *Osaka Isakuro*
Osborne
    Ex: *Cheryl Osborne Sanson*

Osetra
    Ex: *Jenna Osetra Francisco*
Osla
    Ex: *Osla Irvine Iscane*
Oslo
    Ex: *Oslo C Robbins*
Oster
    Ex: *Oster Cates*
Otaki
    Ex: *Otaki Elliko*
Ouzo
    (OO-ZO)
    Ex: *Ouzo Berrin Skolkavinoski*
Ovieda
    Ex: *Ovieda Maria Taranella*
Oviedo
    Ex: *Oviedo Braxton Post*
Oyal
    (OIL)
    Ex: *Oyal Saze Alliston*
Oz
    Ex: *Oz Layton Janes*
Ozark
    Ex: *Sam Ozark Ilands*

Pace
> Ex: *Pace Saunders*

Pacific
> Ex: *Willis Pacific Price*

Pacifica
> Ex: *Pacifica Dino*

Palatino
> Ex: *Palatino Emma Plattes*

Pali
> Ex: *Pali Daston*

Panama
> Ex: *Panama Sails Fellini*

Panna
> Ex: *Panna Cotta Jone*

Para
> Ex: *Para Torrin Tales*

Parade
> Ex: *Parade Orlin Mollison*

Paradise
> Ex: *Anne Paradise Larsen*

Paradiso
> Ex: *Paradiso Pettano*

Paramount
> Ex: *Paramount Christo Revine*

Parish
> Ex: *Maxwell Parish Dores*

Parson
> Ex: *Parson Phillips*

Pasha
> Ex: *Lauranne Pasha Verra*

Pasqua
> Ex: *Pasqua Kara Tates*

Patina
> Ex: *Jaqueline Patina Rave*

Patton
> Ex: *Patton Price*

Pendleton
Ex: *Pendleton Billington*
Pendula
Ex: *Pendula Rachele Wells*
Pennsylvania
Ex: *Pennsylvania C Tycour*
Peralta
Ex: *Peralta Meris Deins*
Perdido
Ex: *Perdido Durango*
Peridot
Ex: *Peridot Yorinsin*
Perrin
Ex: *Perrin Miles*
Peru
Ex: *Bilden Peru Berrin*
Peetes
Ex: *Peetes Wexford*
Petcoff
Ex: *Martin Petcoff Renneski*
Peugeot
(PU-ZJO)
Ex: *Peugeot Spassovski*
Peyton
Ex: *Peyton Rexford*
Phantom
Ex: *Phontom Cains*
Phelps
Ex: *Phelps Norrins*
Philadelphia
Ex: *Philadelphia Parrington*
Phoenix
Ex: *Phoenix Rhodes*
Pico
Ex: *Pico Arroyo*
Piedmont
Ex: *Piedmont Royals*

Pierino
> (P-AIR-EE-NO)
> Ex: *Pierino Venalta*

Pierot
> (P-AIR-OH)
> Ex: *Pierot Salvaggio*

Pilot
> Ex: *Pilot Morriston*

Pilsner
> Ex: *Sayna Pilsner Waynes*

Pitney
> Ex: *Pitney O Thomasson*

Pixel
> Ex: *Pixel Anne Ryerson*

Pixi
> Ex: *Pixi Staten*

Poet
> Ex: *Poet Sites*

Poland
> Ex: *Jori Poland Dayland*

Polaris
> Ex: *Polaris Robbins*

Pomona
> Ex: *Lee Pomona Giffen*

Porter
> Ex: *Porter Saxby*

Powell
> Ex: *Powell Johnson*

Presidio
> Ex: *Presidio Fites*

Price
> Ex: *Price T Walkin*

Quaid
    Ex: *Quaid Chex*
Quebec
    Ex: *Quebec Stevens*
Quill
    Ex: *Quill Fenter Stapleton*
Quillin
    Ex: *Quillin Jerrund Jossens*
Quimby
    Ex: *Quimby Allton*
Quince
    Ex: *Gilda Quince Bayes*
Quinley
    Ex: *Quinley Scott*

Radcliff
>   Ex: *Radcliff Sites*

Rada
>   Ex: *Rada Petcoff*

Rado
>   (REY-DO or RAH-DO)
>   Ex: *Rado Lisson Reeds*

Rainer
>   Ex: *Rainer Janes*

Raines
>   Ex: *Raines Peyton Seyerton*

Ralland
>   Ex: *Ralland Smith*

Ralston
>   Ex: *Ralston Terrence Cartwrighte*

Ramero
>   Ex: *Ramero Bettes*

Ramic
>   Ex: *Ramic Lewis Lynden*

Ramos
>   Ex: *Ramos Vennin*

Rand
>   Ex: *Rand Lock Shorelands*

Rapallo
>   Ex: *Rapallo Bose Nealand*

Rasina
>   Ex: *Rasina Carrie Sattsworth*

Raskin
>   Ex: *Raskin Jones*

Raven
>   Ex: *Raven Marston*

Raydon
>   Ex: *Raydon Poland Rexler*

Raymar
>   Ex: *Raymar Feinland*

Red
>   Ex: *Red Jacks*

Reeves
Ex: *Reeves Kallington*
Regatta
Ex: *Regatta Shelton*
Regent
Ex: *Regent T Moore*
Reidel
(RYE-DELL)
Ex: *Reidel Wakesfield*
Reiland
(RYE-LAND)
Ex: *Reiland Pakkerton*
Rembrandt
Ex: *Rembrandt T Skolanski*
Renida
Ex: *Renida Dakston*
Renoir
Ex: *Renoir Sira Annato*
Renwick
Ex: *Renwick Larkin Casselmar*
Reuse
Ex: *Reuse Baxton*
Revelle
Ex: *Revelle Nera Hennestan*
Reynard
Ex: *Reynard Phillips*
Reznor
Ex: *Reznor Tolland Wellston*
Rhen
Ex: *Leena Rhen Rittsmer*
Rhode
Ex: *Rhode Kellerin*
Rhodes
Ex: *Julan Rhodes Schaler*
Rhodium
Ex: *Rhodium Cyncro*

Rhone
> Ex: *Rhone Stein*

Rialta
> Ex: *Rialta Rose Pirella*

Rialto
> Ex: *Rialto Dino Tellani*

Riata
> (REE-AH-TA)
> Ex: *Riata Sena Merrina*

Rice
> Ex: *Rice Tyemore Cains*

Richmond
> Ex: *Richmond Davis*

Richter
> (RICK-TER)
> Ex: *Richter Ballanski*

Ridley
> Ex: *Ridley Sakes*

Rif
> Ex: *Rif Thomas*

Rio
> Ex: *Rio Corrado*

Ritz
> Ex: *Denna Ritz Westmar*

Riven
> Ex: *Riven Kyle Lirassen*

Rivet
> Ex: *Rivet Jakes*

Riyal
> Ex: *Riyal T Hane*

Robe
> Ex: *Robe Bronstin*

Roble
> Ex: *Roble T Raddisen*

Rock
> Ex: *Rock Milton Edisson*

Rodeo
Ex: *Layton Rodeo Jayez*
Rodin
Ex: *Rodin Sikes*
Roleen
Ex: *Roleen Mirando Cortez*
Romain
Ex: *Julan Romain Merris*
Rondo
Ex: *Rondo Consello*
Ronin
Ex: *Ronin Charton*
Rousseau
Ex: *Rousseau Gaston Morrai*

Royce
Ex: *Royce Silverton*
Rubicon
Ex: *Rubicon Francisco*
Rubine
Ex: *Rubine Rose*
Ruellia
(ROO-EL-EE-UH)
Ex: *Ruellia Marie Sallina*
Rupi
Ex: *Rupi Sans*

Safari
> Ex: *Safari Lange*

Safford
> Ex: *Safford Tye Price*

Saffron
> Ex: *Saffron Julie Lestin*

Sage
> Ex: *Sage Price*

Sahara
> Ex: *Sahara Dray*

Sail
> Ex: *Sail Milts*

Sailes
> Ex: *Sailes Lisa Daye*

Sake
> Ex: *Sake Terrison*

Saks
> Ex: *Mary Saks Westin*

Salem
> Ex: *Salem Shores*

Salen
> Ex: *Salen Eldo Torres*

Salina
> Ex: *Salina Torrentino*

Salinger
> Ex: *Salinger Greene*

Salt
> Ex: *Salt Jeffsen*

Samir
> Ex: *Samir Shabilla*

Sansome
> Ex: *Sansome J Foxner*

Santana
> Ex: *Santana Domingo Vortenya*

Sapphire
> Ex: *Katherine Sapphire Si*

Saran

 Ex: *Saran Marie Deltano*

Saroyan

 Ex: *Saroyan Korani*

Sash

 Ex: *Sash Lucky Cares*

Sashiko

 Ex: *Susan Sashiko Lee*

Saskia

 Ex: *Caroline Saskia Abbott*

Sato

 (SAY-TOW)

 Ex: *Sato Cales Yoshinto*

Sattelite

 Ex: *Sattelite Jino Vallentes*

Sattler

 Ex: *Rick Sattler Sonnes*

Saurus

 Ex: *Saurus Trekk*

Sauterne

 Ex: *Sauterne Reyna Palis*

Savin

 Ex: *Savin Anis Lira*

Savoy

 Ex: *Savoy Rites*

Saxby

 Ex: *Saxby West*

Sayre

 Ex: *Sayre T Jal*

Schale

 Ex: *Schale Kares*

Schell

 Ex: *Laura Schell Wallace*

Scorsese

 (SCORE-SAY-CEE)

 Ex: *James Scorsese Ballacondi*

Scotch
    Ex: *Scotch Braxton*
Seaford
    Ex: *Seaford Miles Vellis*
Seal
    Ex: *Rilford Seal Cansoen*
Seales
    Ex: *Seales Jorr*
Seastar
    Ex: *Vic Seastar Windes*
Sedona
    Ex: *Sam Sedona Prattes*
Seeno
    (C-NO)
    Ex: *Seeno Mani Santorino*

Segal
    Ex: *Segal Grace*
Segovia
    Ex: *Roland Segovia Garcia*
Seiler
    (SAY-LER)
    Ex: *Seiler North*
Seketo
    (SEH-KAY-TOW)
    Ex: *Seketo Nakaru*
Selena
    (SEL-AY-NA)
    Ex: *Selena Ile Cantore*
Sella
    Ex: *Sella Starlin*
Selton
    Ex: *Richard Selton Giles*
Selva
    Ex: *Selva Smith*
Selvet
    Ex: *Selvet Maria Stares*

Seneca
Ex: *Seneca J Williams*
Sential
Ex: *Sential Mary Ferante*
Sephora
Ex: *Sephora Marcia Wills*
Seravando
Ex: *Seravando Costillando*
Serenade
Ex: *Serenade Bastille*
Serin
Ex: *Serin O Wilkens*
Serrano
Ex: *Serrano Callinda*
Serre
Ex: *Serre Talikovsky*
Serrena
Ex: *Serrena Quelannos*
Serrone
Ex: *Serrone Jarin Fellini*
Sesoto
Ex: *Sesoto Ellyn Brochair*
Seton
(CEE-TON)
Ex: *Seton Vaines*
Seuss
Ex: *Carlo Seuss Dexler*
Seven
Ex: *Seven Axel Ace*
Seveno
Ex: *Seveno D Sorrentino*
Shad
Ex: *Shad Weiman Marcson*
Shadow
Ex: *Shadow Weiss*
Sharkey
Ex: *Sharkey Plattes*

Shamiram
> Ex: *Shamiram Ruth Rachele Feinglass*

Sherlock
> Ex: *Rolland Sherlock Calliston*

Shiso
> (SHE-SO)
> Ex: *Shiso Sugato*

Shulamith
> Ex: *Shulamith Sayad*

Shushan
> Ex: *Shushan Sena Venaya*

Silica
> Ex: *Silica Torrentino*

Silver
> Ex: *Silver Trax*

Sin
> Ex: *Sin Sirocco*

Sinclair
> Ex: *Jackson Sinclair Marteno*

Sisal
> (SIGH-SUL)
> Ex: *Sisal Linden Ascot*

Sisiphus
> Ex: *Hale Sisiphus Waldron*

Sistina
> Ex: *Sistina Louisse Mirranta*

Skidmore
> Ex: *Skidmore Chains*

Sky
> Ex: *Sky Ryan Robetson*

Slade
> Ex: *Slade Jones*

Snow
> Ex: *Snow O Holday*

Soire
> (SWAR)
> Ex: *Soire Keats*

Sola
    Ex: *Sola Terra DeCarta*
Solice
    Ex: *Rebecca Solice Rite*
Solin
    Ex: *Solin Marston Bessento*
Solito
    Ex: *Solito Toma Bentayno*
Sonnet
    Ex: *Sonnet Stark*
Sorrell
    Ex: *Sorrell C Axton*
Sota
    Ex: *Sota Phillips*
Sotelo
    Ex: *Sotelo Viso Marketo*

Spanish
    Ex: *Belinda Spanish Illes*
Spano
    (SPA-NO)
    Ex: *Seena Spano Wright*
Spasso
    Ex: *Spasso Ray Gambino*
Spear
    Ex: *Spear C Daye*
Spector
    Ex: *Spector Mardin Ross*
Spenger
    Ex: *Spenger Fishlin*
Sperry
    Ex: *Sperry Halliday*
Spivey
    Ex: *Spivey Ronald Karens*
Spruce
    Ex: *Spruce Wexter*
Ssential
    Ex: *Ssential Lace*

Stafford
>   Ex: *Stafford Seyton*

Stag
>   Ex: *Stag Cortin Foster*

Stallone
>   Ex: *Davin Stallone Costelleno*

Stanislaus
>   Ex: *Leslie Stanislaus Dellanto*

Star
>   Ex: *Jack Star Frost*

Staten
>   Ex: *Staten Jaron Maxton*

Stel
>   Ex: *Stel C Yalene*

Steele
>   Ex: *Steele Dane Lyndon*

Steinbeck
>   Ex: *Hale Steinbeck Reese*

Steiner
>   Ex: *Cole Steiner Waters*

Sting
>   Ex: *Lace Sting Hallen*

Stinson
>   Ex: *Stinson Price*

Stoli
>   Ex: *Stoli Grayson*

Stolich
>   Ex: *Stolich J Montanjo*

Storey
>   Ex: *Storey Constance*

Stylo
>   Ex: *Stylo Peretti*

Sulawesi
>   Ex: *Carmen Salawesi Jay*

Sultana
>   Ex: *Sultana Vey Spassovski*

Sumatra
  Ex: *Sumatra Boran Stelani*
Sumava
  Ex: *Sumava Riyan Allani*
Sumaza
  Ex: *Sumi Sumaza Sise*
Suname
  (SUE-NA-ME)
  Ex: *Bailey Suname Nenzano*
Sutter
  Ex: *Sutter Ray Vilenos*
Sylvania
  Ex: *Lucille Sylvania Pearman*
Syra
  Ex: *Syra Rollans*
Syson
  Ex: *Syson Pakistan*
Syvil
  Ex: *Syvil Kay Tine*

Tabaccan
>   Ex: *Tabaccan Landow*

Tabora
>   Ex: *Tabora Lean Dassin*

Tacoma
>   Ex: *Tacoma Sareen Halen*

Tafati
>   Ex: *Tafati Voyani*

Taipei
>   Ex: *Taipei Nevira*

Taiwan
>   Ex: *Peri Taiwan Rin*

Takoma
>   Ex: *Takoma Rhodes*

Talisker
>   Ex: *Fenton Talisker*

Talkien
>   (TAL-KEY-EN)
>   Ex: *Torren Talkien Wayne*

Talla
>   Ex: *Talla Jeannie Corsaire*

Talon
>   Ex: *Talon Valen Lyte*

Tamarack
>   Ex: *Tamarack Jackson*

Tamarin
>   Ex: *Tamarin Barcowski*

Tamayo
>   Ex: *Tamayo Guterrez*

Tamloren
>   Ex: *Tamloren Phillips*

Tamorino
>   Ex: *Tamorino Jane Tollin*

Tangier
>   Ex: *Angela Tangier Barston*

Targa
>   Ex: *Targa Nellie Dinneo*

Taro
   (TARE-OH)
   Ex: *Taro Katofski*
Tasso
   Ex: *Tasso Yasmine Kaes*
Tatum
   Ex: *Tatum Hilliardson*
Taupe
   Ex: *Taupe Franksen*
Tavin
   Ex: *Tavin J Lawsen*
Tavira
   Ex: *Tavira T Rexton*
Tavito
   Ex: *Freddy Tavito Gaston*
Taxi
   Ex: *Taxi Dae*
Teha
   (TEH-UH)
   Ex: *Teha Jorinski*
Teal
   Ex: *Sean Teal Corman*
Tech
   Ex: *Tech Richards*
Tehama
   Ex: *Tehama Deuno Gonzales*
Tellar
   Ex: *Tellar Axton*
Telly
   Ex: *Telly Lean Viceroy*
Tempela
   Ex: *Annie Tempela Jorlan*
Tennesse
   Ex: *Tennessee Ray*
Teno
   (TAY-NO)
   Ex: *Teno Raston Marker*

T

Teruko
> (TEH-ROO-KO)
>
> Ex: *Teruko Shohara*

Thelonius
> Ex: *Thelonius Mullen*

Tiago
> Ex: *Tiago Martin Rondejo*

Tibet
> Ex: *Tibet C Williamson*

Tice
> Ex: *Tice Jester*

Tide
> Ex: *Karen Tide Kingston*

Tiental
> Ex: *Tiental O Cayne*

Tier
> Ex: *Tier Lily Kates*

Tiller
> Ex: *Tiller Pollen*

Timo
> Ex: *Timo Escar Sevilla*

Tivoli
> Ex: *Tivoli Vince Terrani*

Tobiko
> Ex: *Tobiko Takara*

Tobler
> Ex: *Tobler C Rochanis*

Tohara
> Ex: *Tohara Hamoto*

Tokyo
> Ex: *Toyko Litton*

Toland
> Ex: *Toland Barrister*

Tommaso
> Ex: *Tommaso Paesano*

Tonara
> Ex: *Tonara Loreen Marbella*

Tonic
　　Ex: *Tonic Laston*
Tonix
　　Ex: *Warren Tonix Saitlin*
Toon
　　Ex: *Toon Phillips*
Topeka
　　Ex: *Topeka Anderson*
Torin
　　Ex: *Torin C Alton*
Torina
　　Ex: *Torina Maria Sandara*
Torino
　　Ex: *Torino Cavello Sallenka*
Torious
　　Ex: *Torious Jakes*
Toro
　　Ex: *Astin Toro Kaye*
Toronto
　　Ex: *Toronto Jones*
Totem
　　Ex: *Kyle Totem Wexford*
Town
　　Ex: *Colin Town Akers*
Toy
　　Ex: *Toy Lawson*
Toyon
　　Ex: *Toyon Perrins*
Trinidad
　　Ex: *Trinidad Jakarta*
Trinity
　　Ex: *Trinity Peerson*
Triton
　　Ex: *Triton Phillips*
Triumph
　　Ex: *Triumph Banks*

Trocade
    Ex: *Jenna Trocade Lexington*
Tropic
    Ex: *Tropic T Iles*
Truin
    Ex: *Truin Willit Sallisten*
Tucson
    Ex: *Tucson Delana*
Tule
    Ex: *Westmore Tule Finland*
Tundro
    Ex: *Rootie Tundro Cabintor*
Tustin
    Ex: *Tustin Jamiesen*
Tye
    Ex: *Tye Bansen*
Tyne
    Ex: *Tyne Feldner*

Tzale
    Ex: *Tzale Gin*
Tzena
    Ex: *Tzena O Dio*
Tzeno
    Ex: *Tzeno Mex*
Tzore
    Ex: *Tzore Jenazzo*

Ukiah
> Ex: *Ukiah C Stevens*

Ultraviolet
> Ex: *Ultraviolet Smith*

Uma
> Ex: *Uma Dae*

Uni
> Ex: *Uni Tores*

Uson
> Ex: *Uson Elo Rae*

V
>   Ex: *Perry V Landor*

Vale
>   Ex: *Vale Santos*

Valen
>   Ex: *Valen C Haleston*

Vallarte
>   Ex: *Vallarte Mindez Nirello*

Vallerian
>   Ex: *Vallerian Saston Tull*

Vancouver
>   Ex: *Vancouver Blake*

Vanden
>   Ex: *Vanden C Forriston*

Vanderlin
>   Ex: *Vanderlin Sommers Hale*

Vangough
>   Ex: *Samuel Vangough Li*

Varsi
>   Ex: *Varsi Raddes*

Veany
>   Ex: *Veany Petcoff*

Vecta
>   Ex: *Vecta Sails*

Vector
>   Ex: *Vector T Paston*

Vela
>   Ex: *Vela C Jones*

Vellino
>   Ex: *Vellino Marston*

Velliz
>   Ex: *Velliz Kona Chodroff*

Velna
>   Ex: *Velna Ashford*

Velo
>   Ex: *Velo Martine Vultano*

Velox
>   Ex: *Velox Hay*

Velure
>   Ex: *Velure Barbados*

Velutina
>   Ex: *Velutina Sasskina*

Venetka
>   Ex: *Ventka Petcoff*

Venice
>   Ex: *Venice Bisset Cansora*

Venisson
>   Ex: *Venisson Paynes Price*

Venora
>   Ex: *Venora Helena Fernando*

Veranda
>   Ex: *Veranda Carmine*

Verbena
>   Ex: *Verbena Stills*

Verdict
>   Ex: *Joran Verdict Jones*

Vermont
>   Ex: *Vermont Roden*

Verona
>   Ex: *Verona Addson Sainnes*

Versaille
>   Ex: *Francoise Versaille Poirot*

Vestry
>   Ex: *Lew Vestry Colton*

Vets
>   Ex: *Vets Miller*

Vicari
>   Ex: *Vicari Angelli*

Vidal
>   Ex: *Vidal O Zella*

Vidalia
>   (VY-DAY-LI-UH)
>   Ex: *Vidalia Nellie Stoen*

Video
    Ex: *Video Poland Vice*
Vienna
    Ex: *Vienna Varten Marks*
Viera
    Ex: *Viera DeTano*
Vignette
    Ex: *Silvia Vignette Torena*
Villena
    Ex: *Villena Marie Belinda*
Villian
    Ex: *Max Villian Sine*
Ving
    Ex: *Ving Ellis*
Vinniki
    Ex: *Vinniki Sandokowski*
Vinyl
    Ex: *Vinyl Corman*
Vio
    Ex: *Vio Scallin*
Violeto
    Ex: *Violeto Ristino*
Viper

    Ex: *Jackson Viper Dyce*
Viridine
    Ex: *Viridine Kadir*
Visa
    Ex: *Visa Marie Ossenta*
Visala
    Ex: *Visala Tippes*
Visali
    Ex: *Visali T Celtorres*
Visalia
    Ex: *Raquel Visalia Monroe*
Visino
    Ex: *Visino Esco Voltirez*
Visoko
    Ex: *Visoko Perrino*

Visolo
> Ex: *Visolo Poltani*

Vitaya
> Ex: *Vitaya Reeds*

Vitro
> Ex: *Vitro Hayes*

Vitron
> Ex: *Vitron C Parsen*

Volley
> Ex: *Volley Dayo*

Voxen
> Ex: *Voxen T Morrison*

Wade
    Ex: *Wade Harrison*
Waikawa
    (WHY-KA-WA)
    Ex: *Waikawa Loa*
Waikea
    (WHY-KEY-UH)
    Ex: *Waikea Lani*
Waters
    Ex: *Price Waters Gatelyn*
Waymond
    Ex: *Waymond C Barrister*
Wedge
    Ex: *Wedge Morrison*
Weiland
    (WHY-LIND)
    Ex: *Weiland Price*
Weiler
    (WHY-LER)
    Ex: *Weiler Takston*
Wen
    Ex: *Wen Eston*
Wesson
    Ex: *Wesson Vexler Carrington*
Westcliffe
    Ex: *Westcliffe Borlin*

Westville
    Ex: *Westville Samuel Sinns*
Wexler
    Ex: *Wexler T Bates*
Whitaker
    Ex: *Jallon Whitaker Atkin*
Whitecliff
    Ex: *Whitecliff Bryerson*
Wiana
    Ex: *Wiana Willistine*

Wildes
Ex: *Roscoe Wildes Koh*
Winford
Ex: *Winford Mar Elston*
Winona
Ex: *Winona Rachele Wicksford*
Winrich
Ex: *Winrich Sailes*
Wisconsin
Ex: *Wisconsin Perra Goldberg*
Wolf
Ex: *Wolf Bekks*
Wren
Ex: *Wren Stevens*
Wrex
Ex: *Wrex T Besselton*
Wye
Ex: *Wye Cyland*
Wykosa
Ex: *Wykosa C Shores*
Wylie
Ex: *Wylie Ceyoto*
Wyoming
Ex: *Wyoming Mayes*

Xenium
>   Ex: *Xenium Stone*

Xenon
>   Ex: *Xenon Delirium*

Xeros
>   Ex: *Xeros Kite*

Xray
>   Ex: *Xray Tones*

Xuki
>   Ex: *Xuki Mirres*

Xylene
>   (ZY-LEEN)
>   Ex: *Xylene Aced*

Xylia
>   Ex: *Xylia Lane*

Xylo
>   Ex: *Xylo Sarres*

Xylose
>   Ex: *Xylose Deorta*

Yacht
>Ex: *Tara Yacht Walton*

Yamoto
>Ex: *Yamoto Yoshiro*

Yana
>Ex: *Yana J Broughten*

Yare
>Ex: *Yare Julus Astin*

Yeager
>Ex: *Yeager Tuldanich*

Yemen
>Ex: *Yemen Roconovitch*

Yolano
>Ex: *Yolano Deisina*

Yosemite
>Ex: *Yosemite Payes*

Yoshi
>Ex: *Yoshi Itano*

Yoshiko
>Ex: *Yoshiko Uchida*

Ysina
>Ex: *Ysina Marks*

Yucatan
>Ex: *Yucatan Ides*

Yukon
>Ex: *Yukon Orlands*

Yunnan
>Ex: *Yunnan Seeres*

Zagat
>Ex: *Zagat Emillsen*

Zahara
>Ex: *Zahara Jolie*

Zahir
>Ex: *Zahir Rhodani*

Zahlia
>(ZAY-LEE-AH)
>Ex: Zahlia Madrid

Zaire
>Ex: *Zaire Aldens*

Zala
>Ex: *Zala Johnson*

Zale
>Ex: *Zale Corrinsko*

Zamora
>Ex: *Zamora Jones*

Zanella
>Ex: *Zanella Ferrintino*

Zarim
>Ex: *Zarim Khyan*

Zarina
>Ex: *Zarina Elline Wayla*

Zarino
>Ex: *Zarino Bestorre*

Zarzuela
>Ex: Zarzuela Varendo

Zax
>Ex: *Zax Baxford*

Zealand
>Ex: *Zealand Stanton*

Zealander
>Ex: Zealander Valor

Zein
>Ex: *Zein Wints*

Zena
>Ex: *Zena Seiles*

Zeni
>(ZEE-NEE)
>Ex: *Zeni Jetkin*

Zenith
>Ex: *Zenith Warrens*

Zeo
>Ex: *Zeo Beilind*

Zeppli
>Ex: *Zeppli Rhodes*

Zepplin
>Ex: *Zepplin J Doberlin*

Zimara
>Ex: Zimara Allende

Zimbabwe
>Ex: *Charlin Zimbabwe Moldeno*

Zimbor
>Ex: *Restin Zimbor Kales*

Zinc
>Ex: *Zinc Erriden*

Zinnia
>Ex: *Rachele Zinnia Larres*

Zipper
>Ex: *Zipper Kates*

Zircon
>Ex: *Zircon Tolberts*

Zirrinia
>Ex: *Zirrinia Leiberts*

Zito
>Ex: *Zito Martinello*

Ziziva
>Ex: *Ziziva Sonnet*

Zodiak
>Ex: *Seyla Zodiak Basin*

Zoot
>Ex: *Zoot Maxton*

Zuki
> Ex: *Zuki Barrington*

Zuni
> Ex: *Zuni Wilsen*

Zurich
> Ex: *Zurich Moreno*

VALERIE HANSEN

The author with **Reznor Tolland Tyler Wellston**

3 6645 00049962 4 ✓

929.44
D
    David, Daniel.

      The complete book of
      unusual names.

DATE			

$11.95

929.44
D
    David, Daniel.

      The complete book of
      unusual names.

BAKER & TAYLOR